WALKING

—

LUNESDALE

WALKING COUNTRY

———

LUNESDALE

Paul Hannon

———

Hillside

HILLSIDE
PUBLICATIONS
20 Wheathead Crescent
Keighley
West Yorkshire
BD22 6LX

First published 2009

© Paul Hannon 2009

ISBN 978-1-870141-93-2

Cover illustration: Devil's Bridge, Kirkby Lonsdale
Back cover: Middleton Fell; Low Bentham; Crook o'Lune
Page One: Waterfalls on Leck Beck
Page Three: Sundial, Low Bentham
(Paul Hannon/Hillslides Picture Library)

The sketch maps in this book are based upon
1947 Ordnance Survey One-Inch maps

Printed in Great Britain by
Carnmor Print
95-97 London Road
Preston
Lancashire
PR1 4BA

CONTENTS

INTRODUCTION

Lunesdale is a beautiful, highly accessible pocket of walking country running from the Yorkshire Dales to Lancaster, with the scenic market town of Kirkby Lonsdale at its heart. The River Lune rises on the northern slopes of the Howgill Fells, but rather than flow northwards to the Eden it loops around their base to emerge near Sedbergh. The country between here and Lancaster - beyond which it enters the sea - is the rewarding location of these walks. Updale from Kirkby the Lune neatly marks the western limit of the Yorkshire Dales, flowing between the majestic rolling country of Middleton and Casterton Fells on its east bank and unfrequented parkland to the west. Downstream, meanwhile, the Lune flows wide and calm, absorbing the side valleys of the Greta and the Wenning flowing from the fringes of the Dales and Bowland.

In this richly diverse area you can move easily from bracing fellwalk to riverside ramble. The walks encounter charming villages such as Barbon, Wray and Burton-in-Lonsdale, and individual delights such as the Devil's Bridge, Leck Beck and the Crook o'Lune. Variety of surroundings is equalled by variety of location: the upper dale falls within Cumbria, below Kirkby is Lancashire, while the eastern tributaries flow from North Yorkshire.

Centrepiece of the district is Kirkby Lonsdale, the 'church in the Lune Valley'. This delightful little town sits high above the river and is a perfect base for exploration. Focal point is the market square, from which streets of shops, pubs and cafes radiate. The church of St Mary the Virgin dates from the 12th century, and though largely hidden from view it boasts its own excellent views, as an octagonal gazebo looks out over the Lune. Turner painted this view and Ruskin enthused over it: a path lets you do likewise en route to the town's best known feature, Devil's Bridge.

Access to the countryside

The majority of walks in this guide are on public rights of way with no access restrictions. Walks 3, 4 and 6 take advantage of Open Access: on most days of the year you are free to walk over these wonderful landscapes, though in reality they have long been responsibly enjoyed. Further information can be obtained from the Countryside Agency, and ideally from information centres.

Using the guide

Each walk is self-contained, with essential information being followed by a concise route description and simple map. Dovetailed in between are notes and illustrations of features along the way. Snippets of information have been placed in *italics* to ensure that the essential route description is easier to locate. The sketch maps serve to identify the location of the routes rather than the fine detail, and whilst the description should be sufficient to guide you around, an Ordnance Survey map is strongly recommended.

To gain the most from a walk, the detail of the 1:25,000 scale Explorer map is unsurpassed. It also gives the option to vary walks as desired, giving an improved picture of your surroundings and the availability of linking paths. Just two maps cover all the walks:
• *Explorer OL2 - Yorkshire Dales South/West*
• *Explorer OL41 - Forest of Bowland & Ribblesdale*
Useful for planning is Landranger map 97 (and a tiny bit of map 98)

USEFUL ADDRESSES

Ramblers' Association
2nd Floor, Camelford House, 87-89 Albert Embankment, London SE1 7BR
• 020-7339 8500
Tourist Information
24 Main Street **Kirkby Lonsdale** LA6 2AE • 015242-71437
29 Castle Hill **Lancaster** LA1 1YN • 01524-32878
Community Centre **Ingleton** LA6 3HG • 015242-41049
Town Hall, Highgate **Kendal** LA9 4DL • 01539-725758
Town Hall, Station Rd **Bentham** LA2 7LH • 015242-62549 (seasonal)
Open Access
Helpline • 0845-100 3298, *or* www.countrysideaccess.gov.uk
Public Transport Information
Traveline • 0870 608 2608 National Rail Enquiries • 08457-484950

Left: the Roman milestone, Middleton

1

AROUND MIDDLETON

START Rigmaden   Grid ref. SD 617848

DISTANCE $5\frac{3}{4}$ miles (9km)

ORDNANCE SURVEY MAPS
1:50,000
Landranger 97 - Kendal & Morecambe
1:25,000
Explorer OL2 - Yorkshire Dales South/West

ACCESS Start from Rigmaden Bridge on the Old Town road off the Kirkby Lonsdale-Sedbergh road. Verge parking on the east side.

> Exploring the scattered parish of Middleton by fields, farms and lanes, with a good dose of history and big views

Rigmaden Bridge is an uninspiring structure but is, somewhat surprisingly, the only crossing of the Lune between Killington and Kirkby Lonsdale: it also gives a lovely view of the graceful river backed by the Howgill Fells. Don't cross the bridge but head east towards the junction with the main road. *As the wooded bank ends, revealed ahead is the entire girth of Middleton Fell.* Just yards before the main road take the hedgerowed, grassy track of Low Lane on the left, later broadening to lead to a farm road. Go left on this to Hawking Hall, and entering the farmyard bear right to a gate at the corner. A rough track heads away beneath a wooded bank, with Middleton church visible ahead.

When the bank ends you will see the distinctive pillar of a Roman milestone on the brow just ahead. *Unearthed in 1836 and neatly cylindrical, it rises to almost six feet, and its original inscription has been joined by Victorian additions (featured on page 6).* Your route crosses the flat field to the right-hand gate in the fence opposite, then bears right to a gate/stile to the right of the church. Joining the main road go left to the church. *With its single bell-cote Middleton's isolated church of the Holy Ghost dates from 1879, on the site of earlier chapels.*

Continue along the road for a short while. *Part way on is an old milestone, its 'S5, KL 5³4' indicating mileages to Sedbergh and Kirkby Lonsdale.* Just beyond it is a junction where you can escape right on a narrow back lane. *One minute further on the main road (a former Roman road) is the temptingly located Swan Inn. Middleton also boasts another pub, The Head, a mile and a half further along the road.* The back road runs to a junction at High Stockdale Bridge at High Green.

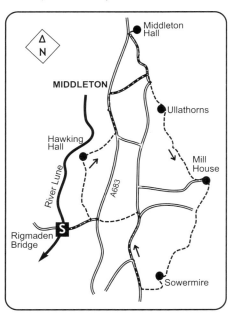

Though the onward route turns right here, consider a virtual mile-long round detour left on this narrow back road to the main road again, where stands Middleton Hall (it's included in the mileage!). *The effort repays you with a stroll up the drive to appraise the magnificent, massive curtain wall with its arched gateway framing the 15th century house, still a working farm.*

Your onward route is right, briefly, until the little lane swings sharp right where you take a wall-stile on the left. *Throughout this section you are rambling just beneath the open flanks of Middleton Fell.* Rise across the field to a corner gate, then cross to one into the farmyard at Ullathorns. Noting the house with its 1617 datestone, turn right on the drive out. When it swings right to the road, take a gate in front and head off along the wallside, through another gate and on to a corner, where slant left up to Tossbeck. From a gate into the yard, turn left between the buildings to leave by a rail underpass. *This is the former Clapham-Lowgill line which traced the Lune Valley via Sedbergh to meet the main line at Tebay. It was opened by the Lancaster & Carlisle Railway Company in 1861, and just saw its centenary before closure in 1964.*

The Lune at Rigmaden

Rising into a field, bear right along the bottom edge to a stile onto an access road. From the stile opposite slant left to a stile in a tumbledown wall, then on again to a corner gate in a dip. A wall-stile just behind sees you maintain this line, rising to a well hidden wall-stile in the corner just ahead. Slant up a bigger field to a gate in the fence above, just yards short of the corner, then on again to a stile onto a surfaced access road. Rise left to Mill House, passing through a gate to the holiday cottages above. From a wall-stile between them a little path drops down to a tiny bridge on Millhouse Beck. *This chirpy stream is a good place to linger for a break.* Continue to a barn just ahead, then bear right, briefly, down a stony little track to a gateway in the wall beneath a second barn. *This is a superbly well-preserved, traditional old barn.*

From the gateway cross a large open pasture to approach Low Fellside which soon appears ahead: towards the end you'll see a distinctive wall-stile waiting in line with the house. Advance on, keeping left of the house to a corner gate above the buildings. Continue past a barn and down to a small gate in the fence ahead. Drop right to a gate just below, then turn left along the fieldside. On through a wall-stile and gate, at the end turn right with a wall to pass a barn: in the corner below, a track heads away from the gate. *Prominent up to the left is the landmark cairn on Eskholme Pike.* Across the field the track becomes enclosed to run alongside a rail embankment. An underpass at the end puts you into the yard at Sowermire Farm. At the house turn left on the driveway out, which curves down onto the narrow High Road. Turn right, running peacefully on and keeping right at a junction. Just a minute after bearing left at a fork, take a gate/stile on the left. Cross the long field centre to a stile at the end, and continue away with a hedge, dropping down through a gap-stile and along to a stile back onto the main road junction. With the big house of Rigmaden Park directly ahead over the valley, cross straight over to finish.

Curtain wall, Middleton Hall

2

MANSERGH & RIGMADEN

START *Old Town   Grid ref. SD 595829*

DISTANCE *5³4 miles (9km)*

ORDNANCE SURVEY MAPS
1:50,000
Landranger 97 - Kendal & Morecambe
1:25,000
Explorer OL2 - Yorkshire Dales South/West

ACCESS *Start from the centre of the hamlet on the B6254 Kirkby Lonsdale-Kendal road. Roadside parking.*

Easy walking on old tracks and byways in an unsung corner, enjoying extensive views across to the Lunesdale fells

Though no more than a hamlet, Old Town is the centre of the scattered parish of Mansergh, pronounced 'Manser'. Appropriately enough it enjoys views that will dominate the walk, looking across the Lune Valley to the Howgill Fells, Middleton Fell, Great Coum and Casterton Fell. Head south on the road out, passing the old village pump. Beyond the last house the road rises away, but before the brow take a wall-stile on the left at the end of the first field. Through this descend the wallside, at the bottom corner bearing right with it (not as per map) to slant down to a fence-stile and then a gate onto a track serving the wooden chalets of Lune Valley Park. Cross the grassed area opposite to a stile in front of Hawkrigg farmhouse, and turn right through the yard.

At the end advance straight on through a gate and along a hedgerowed track, quickly transforming into a grassy bridleway. This runs pleasantly along to emerge back onto the B6254, where turn left. *Shortly after Deansbiggin Tram Plantation starts, note an old milestone on the right: simply inscribed '10' and '2', these refer to the distances to Kendal and Kirkby Lonsdale.* Just 120 yards beyond a junction the true right of way departs left through a gap in the beech hedge, but its crossing of part wooded and bracken terrain is blocked: better to trace a path parallel with the road to a driveway just a little further. Turn left down this to the farm of Deansbiggin, keeping left of the house. Remain on the firm track past a series of barns before descending a pleasant hedgerowed course onto a back road. *During this the view to Barbon and Casterton Fells quickly expands to include Middleton Fell and the Howgill Fells.*

Go left for a few quiet minutes along the road to approach Mansergh Hall. *This ordinary looking farmhouse has a farm shop and a fine backdrop of fells.* Level with its drive bear left up the enclosed cart track of Chapel Lane. This rises away to run a grand course, with Old Town over to the left and Mansergh church appearing ahead. At the end a gate puts you into a field. *The eastern panorama reaches from the Howgill Fells ahead all the way back to Bowland.* Continue with the old hedge on your left to a gate at the end. The faint old way then crosses a field centre to a gate left of the church, onto its short driveway. *St Peter's church dates from 1880, and occupies an*

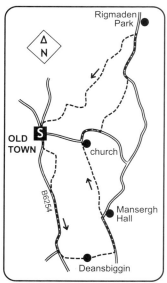

enviable if isolated setting. Advance on to the road just ahead. *Alongside is the old school of 1839, now a private residence.*

Bear right along the narrow road which turns sharp right and drops down to a farm, The Birks. From a gate on the left a good cart track heads off across unkempt pasture. Through a gate at the end it continues in similar surrounds, and from a further gate it crosses to one onto the previous back road. Go left, entering the environs of Rigmaden Park. The elegant house itself soon appears on a mound directly ahead. *This fine mansion was built in 1825 for the Wilson family.* Just before reaching it take a gate on the left and double back up through parkland on a track rising to a gate into Hag Wood. The track runs to the derelict house of Woodside.

After the house rise right to a gate, and curve up with the fence before slanting across to the higher of two gates in the fence rising away. *Look back for a fine prospect of the Howgill Fells.* From it head away with the wall and on past a barn. *Stunningly expansive views have the long Bowland moors skyline beyond the Lune, while Barbon village features across a rare visible section of river.* Beyond a gate, an easily missed variation sees the way enter a narrow, hedgerowed section before meeting the more obvious line at the field end, where through a gate they merge to join Mansergh High's farm drive just ahead.

Go straight on the drive, and as it drops to the farm advance straight on a track to a cluster of barns. Here a slim, enclosed path takes over, running a splendid course with open views to the left. Rising gently to a brow, Old Town appears over to the right. Just before it starts to drop away leave by a squeezer-stile on the right, and follow the wall away to rise outside a tiny wood. Continue on with the wall through a gate, and just before the corner beyond take a gap-stile in the wall and follow the hedge away.

Barbon Low Fell and Casterton Fell from Mansergh church

For your final panorama enthuse over another fine picture, embracing Middleton Fell, Crag Hill, Barbon village, Barbon Low Fell, Casterton Fell, Mansergh church, and a long Bowland skyline along to Clougha Pike. When the hedge ends bear right down the field to locate a wall-stile between an iron gate and the field corner. Turn right to a gate in the wall ahead, and cross the field centre to a wall-stile at the house at Greenbank. Advance on the lawned enclosure to another such stile out onto a roughish back road, the Old Scotch Road. The main road through Old Town is just a minute to the left. *At the junction is an old turnpike milestone inscribed 'Kirkby Lonsdale 3, Kendal 9', with the enterprising inclusion of the 253 miles to London.*

Milestone at Old Town

St Peter's church, Mansergh

15

3

MIDDLETON FELL

START Barbon   Grid ref. SD 628825

DISTANCE $7^1/2$ miles (12km)

ORDNANCE SURVEY MAPS
1:50,000
Landranger 97 - Kendal & Morecambe
Landranger 98 - Wensleydale & Upper Wharfedale
1:25,000
Explorer OL2 - Yorkshire Dales South/West

ACCESS Start from the village centre. Car park at the village hall.
•OPEN ACCESS - see page 7.

> *An emphatic leg-stretcher encircling the wide open
> spaces of this unsung mountain: a real tonic*

The unassuming village of Barbon nestles in a fine Lune Valley
setting, tucked away at the foot of the Dales' westernmost fells.
In spite of its enviable location it is a 'tourist free' area: old
Westmorland lingers on here. Its features include St Bartholomew's
church of 1893, the homely Barbon Inn, a shop, an old Wesleyan
chapel and a former reading room of 1884. Centrepiece is the war
memorial on which the Shuttleworths of Barbon Manor feature
prominently. A narrow road squeezes through the hills to emerge
into the heart of Dentdale.

From the memorial leave the village by the road past the pub
and the church, then turning left along the drive into Barbon Park.
Across the bridge on Barbon Beck the drive swings right to climb to
Barbon Manor, but keep straight on over the grass to pass the top
end of a wood. From the gate at the end keep on to the buildings
at Eskholme, then turn sharp right to ascend to a gate at the top.

This is the last one until you pass back through it to finish. The ascent begins in earnest with the first objective being the cairn on Eskholme Pike: a choice of routes awaits. Either make a direct, steeper pull up short-cropped grass, passing on the way a natural stone chair, the slab of Devil's Crag, and a stone shelter: a thin trod forms part way up. A gentler route takes the grassy quad track slanting left from the gate: when it runs left take the continuing slighter one ahead, slanting up the fell with ease to the base of stonier ground. It swings right here to rise as a thinner way, climbing to fade on a mildly stony shelf. From here bear right to cross to the big cairn on the rocky plinth of Eskholme Pike. *Eskholme Pike is highly prominent from below, and when attained it well merits a halt to survey a superb Lune Valley panorama.*

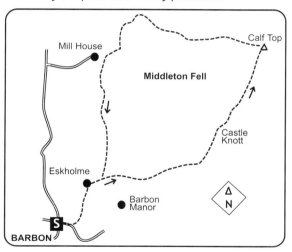

Behind the cairn a trod sets an obvious course along the crest of the grassy ridge, broadening into a quad track. Visible ahead is the cairn on Castle Knott, some way off and still some way short of the main summit. The slope eases further before a mildly stiffer pull, the path occasionally thinning slightly before gaining a tidy cairn. *The bulk of Great Coum looms ahead now across unseen Barbondale.* Passing above a clutch of tiny pools the path swings left beneath grassy knolls, and up ahead the top of Castle Knott beckons. A level section precedes the very short pull, noting an old stone sheepfold on a rash of stones across to the left. On gaining Castle Knott's cairn at 1765ft/538m, a surprise is in store in the form of a substantial depression interrupting the march to Calf Top, Middleton Fell's summit. *The environs of Castle Knott offer some dramatic views over Barbondale to Rise Hill, Baugh Fell, Widdale Fell and Great Coum, while more crucially your summit is at least now visible!* A briefly steep drop becomes slightly faint on the saddle, where a short moist section awaits. A peaty section amid heather precedes a grand pull on a broad path to gain the summit ridge. An old wall/fence corner is reached before the summit, and it guides a simple stroll along to the Ordnance Survey column.

At 1998ft/609m Middleton Fell - or Fells, as the mass is some-times known - is very much a detached parcel of upland, largely outwith the Dales National Park as a result of its allegiance to old Westmorland. Few walkers venture here, thanks in part to its lack of (literally) inches. Resembling the Howgill Fells in character, its occasional slaty outcrops perhaps stand best comparison with Black Combe in the southern Lake District: its slatiness is matched by its deeply incised western gills, its heather flanks, its isolation, and even its happy 'limitations' of altitude (despite which, up here you will feel exceedingly high and remote!). The summit, known as Calf Top, grants extensive views over the north-west counties: a step over the fence gives access to a contrasting close-up view down its sheer east flank, and also puts you inside the National Park. Westwards are Morecambe Bay and an extensive Lakeland skyline, northwards are Sedbergh and the Howgill Fells, while closer still is Dentdale in its surround of sombre fells.

Whilst the obvious option is the pleasurable task of retracing steps (better in poor weather), consider a circular route. Bear west directly away from the summit over barely declining ground. Part way along this shoulder a broad grass track comes in from the right, and will remain your route all the way down to the intake wall. It runs past a small pool, over a slight rise and on to reveal a 7ft stone pillar just 30 yards to the left. The track commences a splendid descent with outstanding Lunesdale views, later entering patches of scattered heather and maintaining a generally straight line down to a more defined edge, with a tiny cairn on a knoll to the right. The second half of the descent starts here. *The Howgill Fells remain in view to the right, with Barbon down the valley.* The way drops a little more steeply but quickly fades: it can be picked up by dropping right to revive in a flatter, grassy area. Here it starts a level run to the right: you can soon short-cut this by dropping down alongside a tiny stream through sparse bracken. Within two minutes the track comes back in from the right, crossing the stream and continuing as a mercurial green way slanting down the bracken-clad fellside. It takes you all the way to the base of the fell, only emerging from bracken two minutes above the intake wall.

Don't go right down to the wall but bear left to the foot of the tree-lined ravine of Millhouse Gill, beneath a super waterfall. Cross and rise briefly with the intake wall, then tramp a nice level course above the wall. As it drops away bear left to the top corner of a wall ahead. Continue atop this, with Eskholme Pike appearing

ahead, and at the end a green path drops down into bracken. Veer left to contour across beneath the bracken limit, ignoring the lower intake wall and crossing over easy ground to the plantation corner ahead. On past it, don't rush to join the wall but use sheeptrods on better terrain before you gravitate towards the wall on good turf, soon reaching the gate back off the fell.

Waterfalls, Millhouse Gill

4

BARBON LOW FELL

START Barbon   Grid ref. SD 628825

DISTANCE 5³4 miles (9km)

ORDNANCE SURVEY MAPS
1:50,000
Landranger 97 - Kendal & Morecambe
Landranger 98 - Wensleydale & Upper Wharfedale (tiny section)
1:25,000
Explorer OL2 - Yorkshire Dales South/West

ACCESS Start from the village centre. Car park at the village hall.
•OPEN ACCESS - see page 7.

A stunning combination of first-rate Dales scenery, and though every step is outside the Dales, it's a National Park landscape

For a note on Barbon see page 16. From the memorial leave the village by the road past the pub and the church, turning left along the drive into Barbon Park. Across the bridge on Barbon Beck the drive swings right to climb to Barbon Manor, but when it swings sharp left away from the beck's wooded environs, a sign indicates a green track heading right to a gate into the trees. Lively Barbon Beck is followed all the way through deep woodland, enjoying beck scenery of the highest order. A big stone-arched bridge is reached where a broader track is met. Bear left on this, rising away from the beck and on to a gate out of the trees. The splendid track runs a grand course through bracken along the base of the steep fell, with the beck below and Barbon Low Fell across it: ahead is the high wall of Crag Hill. At the end, beyond an intervening gate, is a pair of gates alongside a sheepfold. *This is a lovely spot, looking over the confluence of Aygill with Barbon Beck amid tilted rocks.*

Just a little further, a footbridge conveys you to the road on the other side, opposite Fell House farm drive. Turn right a short way with the beck, then rising to crossing Aygill at Blindbeck Bridge. Little over a hundred yards further take a second green way sloping back up to the left. *This climb offers fine views north to the long wall of Middleton Fell.* This grand old bridle-path scales the lower contours of Barbon Low Fell, absorbing the earlier track to ease out on gentler ground. *Gragareth's long skyline appears ahead now.* The track runs on to a gate where it becomes enclosed. *Just prior to this Aygill breaks into a ravine that merits a detour through the gate/stile on the left.*

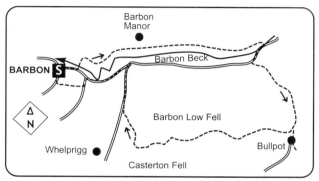

Your onward route doesn't pass through onto the lane, which does however offer a detour to Bullpot Farm. Bullpot is Mecca for denizens of the underground: it has long been the base of the Red Rose Caving Club, and is in great demand as a cavers' bothy. The reason is the proximity of some of the finest cave systems in the land. A detour to see Bullpot's hole might quickly be made. A gate at the end of the house is the key to the cavers' path along the wallside to Bull Pot of the Witches. This dark, forbidding hole drops some 200 feet: wet spells see a waterfall pouring over the lip, though it is easier to hear than see - in safety, at least.

Without passing through the gate turn up the near side of the wall to remain on open fell. Ascend this grassy slope, remaining largely with the wall, with intermittent sheeptrods further easing progress. Beneath telegraph wires you rise to a knoll, then on again with a stony edge over to the right. Another minor knoll is gained to earn big views ahead. *The various knolls of Barbon Low Fell and adjoining Casterton Fell are foreground to a distant panorama of the Lakeland Fells.* A tiny descent sends you off again, a fairly level meander on trods to rise to the highest point of the walk at some 1410ft/430m on a welcoming green knoll just yards up from the wall. *Linger over this splendid viewpoint: on parade are Bowland, Casterton Fell, Morecambe Bay, Hutton Roof Crags, Farleton Fell, the Lakeland Fells across the Lune Valley, Lambrigg Fell (sadly identifiable courtesy of its wind turbines), Whinfell, Middleton Fell, Barbondale, Baugh Fell, Rise Hill, Crag Hill and Gragareth.*

Resume and descend close by the wall, neatly evading the large Nanslope Moss and then on to a minor knoll. This overlooks a more appreciable drop to a hollow. Descend pleasant slopes then follow a trod (keeping away from the wall) along a gentle ridge to approach a wall junction. *Casterton Fell is carpeted with heather over the wall ahead.* Swing right with the wall, on a thin trod shadowing it round two bends to neatly avoid a marsh. Striding the outflow at a tidy confluence, just ahead a fence replaces the wall and the stream transforms into a broadening ravine.

Middleton Fell from Barbon Low Fell

This good little path traces it down steeper slopes, only fading in bracken at the bottom. Pass a large old sheepfold and down to a smaller one across the tiny beck. Behind the fold a grass track runs left through bracken, shadowing the little stream then bearing right and fading a little on grass. *Below is the big house of Whelprigg, while splendid Lune Valley views soon open out.* Swinging right away from the main beck the track quickly reforms in bracken, and as a superb green way it slants all the way down the bracken fellside to an unfenced road along the base of the fell.

Turn right, taking advantage of some good verges. *Round a slight bend the rather grand Barbon Manor appears in the trees ahead: it was built in 1863 as shooting lodge for Sir James Kay-Shuttleworth.* Cut a corner of the junction at the end, turning left over the cattle-grid to drop back into the village, which is revealed only at the last moment. When it does appear, at a minor side road, consider a nicer finish by turning briefly left on this grass stripped lane, then quickly right down an enclosed bridleway (Watery Lane), embowered in greenery. At the bottom it bridges the old railway line and runs as a green way down onto an access road. Just ahead is a junction with a through road, turning right into the centre.

St Bartholomew's church, Barbon

5

AROUND CASTERTON

START *Barbon   Grid ref. SD 628825*

DISTANCE *6¹4 miles (10km)*

ORDNANCE SURVEY MAPS
1:50,000
Landranger 97 - Kendal & Morecambe
1:25,000
Explorer OL2 - Yorkshire Dales South/West

ACCESS *Start from the village centre. Car park at the village hall.*

> *Two neighbouring villages linked by pleasant fieldpaths,*
> *and an encounter with the banks of the Lune*

For a note on Barbon see page 16. From the war memorial leave the village along the side road past the shop and village hall to where the road bends right. Here take a side road left, running a short course towards scattered houses. As it double sharply back right go straight on past the house and up to find yourself on the old railway. *This is the former Clapham-Lowgill line which traced the Lune Valley via Sedbergh to meet the main line at Tebay. It was opened by the Lancaster & Carlisle Railway Company in 1861, and just saw its centenary before closure in 1964.*

Take a small gate above and up a small wooded bank to a kissing-gate into a field. *Up above is the imposing house of Underfell, appropriately named given that Barbon Low Fell's bracken slopes rise behind.* Slant right to rise to a gate onto a narrow back road. Take the stile opposite, a single slab neatly bridging a tiny stream and along the wallside to a pair of gates beneath a belt of trees. With the farm of Low Bank House ahead, bear left to a stile just above it, and go left on a cart track. *There is a good view of Barbon*

Manor nestling in dense trees over to the left under Castle Knott.
This swings round to the right to a gate/stile into a sloping pasture.
A grassy way heads off through reeds, but as the hedge on your
right swings away, instead bear gently left, crossing to find a
gate/stile in the fence ahead. Well before this the mansion of
Whelprigg (1834) will have appeared above. *At the stile you'll see
its walled ha-ha just above you.* Cross the drive to a stile opposite.

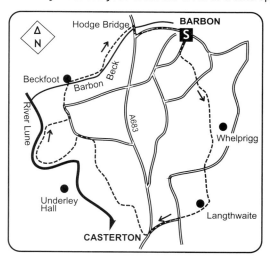

Head away, rising gently to a gate in the wall ahead. Follow
the adjacent fence away, passing through several gates and
deflecting right of sheep pens to a gate onto another back road at
Fell Garth. Cross straight over to a gap-stile and along a garden
edge to a slab crossing a tiny stream. From the little gate behind,
cross to a wall-stile then swing right to a gate, from where a path
runs between new plantings to Hole House. Don't take the gate into
its garden but use the stile alongside and head away with the wall.
A fence soon deflects you up above it and along to a gate/stile
overlooking houses at Langthwaite. *Enjoy big views to the Bowland
moors ahead, with Hutton Roof Crags and Farleton Fell further
right.* Keep on to a stile onto a rough track, turning down it to

absorb the houses' drives: becoming surfaced, it descends to a crossroads. *Here you meet the Roman road from Manchester to Carlisle.* Go straight over and under a defunct rail bridge, and the rough little road runs quickly on to drop past Casterton School and onto the main road alongside the church.

Casterton village is dominated by its girls' school, established in 1833 by Rev William Carus Wilson and considerably expanded in succeeding years. The church of the Holy Trinity was built for the school at the same time. Also centrally placed is the Pheasant Inn. Cross straight over to a slender stile, and a snicket drops between gardens onto an access road at school buildings. Cross straight over, passing between them and up onto another driveway, crossing the main way to run between sports fields to a gate ahead. *There is a good view of Casterton Fell to the right: ahead is a large house, The Grange.* Resume along the fieldside, a grassy way forming to drop left to a gate in a dip. Through it the way rises gently with the wall, The Grange now well seen on your right. Through two gates take one on the left and head along the fieldside towards trees ahead. This pleasant walk runs to the corner, turning right outside further woods to a stile at the end. *Massive views open out over Lunesdale, with the Middleton, Barbon and Casterton Fells to the right and the shapely Howgill Fells ahead. Underley Hall appears as a gaunt pile over the river down to the left: built in the 1820s for the Earl of Bective, it now functions as a school.*

Ignore a stile on the left at the wood corner just ahead, and cross the field to a ladder-stile over a wall. This same course is maintained through good sheep pastures all the way to a road, crossing to an outer wall corner ahead, then alongside it to a gate in an inner corner, crossing to the other side and along to a gate onto Lowfields Lane. Go left, enjoying the company of a lively stream in the woods, and the road drops to a bend. Just to the right it is bridged by a driveway to Underley Hall. Your route, however, takes some steps on the left, and a path runs through trees above a solitary house and down to a stile into a big tract of parkland. Go left with the fence enclosing the wood until crossing a small water-course, then bear right to merge with a track alongside a fence, with the wide-flowing River Lune just across it.

Bear right on here to reach a massive, ornate stone-arched bridge carrying the Underley driveway. Resume beyond it, and a step-stile further along finally puts you onto the true riverbank, with a ladder-stile just beyond. A grand little path now provides the finest section. Enjoy this until beneath overhead power lines, where you reach the site of an old ford. Ignoring a pointless ladder-stile just behind, take the gate on the right and head away from the river. When the accompanying fence bends off, cross the field to the right of the cottages at Low Beckfoot. Joining another drive go left on this out onto the previous road again.

Go left past the cottages, and as the road swings sharp right at a junction take the unsigned branch straight ahead. This runs to cross lively Barbon Beck at High Beckfoot. *Upstream is a charming 17th century packhorse bridge.* Fork right into the yard at Beckfoot Farm and pass the house to a gate. A gentle track heads upstream through colourful surrounds, soon opening out and fading. Simply remain near the beck to a stile at the far end, where a path rises onto a golf course. Advance to a plantation just ahead and follow its right side, just past the end of which an old, enclosed bridleway is met. Turn right on this to reach the beck again. Whilst bridleway users must ford the beck, your route simply resumes upstream, still along the edge of the course and concluding with a short stroll to a wall-stile left of a gate ahead. This puts you onto the A683, turn right to cross stone-arched Hodge Bridge. *Note the old stone guide-post at the corner (see page 5).* With Barbon Beck for company, turn along the side road into the village.

The old railway line at Casterton

6

LECK BECK

START *Cowan Bridge*   *Grid ref. SD 635764*

DISTANCE *6^{1}4 miles (10km)*

ORDNANCE SURVEY MAPS
1:50,000
Landranger 97 - Kendal & Morecambe
Landranger 98 - Wensleydale & Upper Wharfedale (tiny section)
1:25,000
Explorer OL2 - Yorkshire Dales South/West

ACCESS *Start from the village centre. There is a car park up the side road behind the shop. Served by Settle-Kirkby Lonsdale bus.*
•OPEN ACCESS - see page 7.

> *The lovely environs of Leck Beck penetrate unfrequented fell country to discover limestone ravines, all within Lancashire!*

Cowan Bridge is a tiny village astride a busy main road. It boasts a shop, a Methodist chapel and a couple of old boundary stones. The old bridge itself Is sidelined by a modern replacement: alongside is the former Clergymen's Daughters School attended by four of the Bronte sisters in 1824-25. From the main road bridge over Leck Beck, take a stile on the village side and head upstream to pass under an arch of a low viaduct. *The former Clapham-Tebay line ran via the Lune Valley and Sedbergh to the main line at the Lune Gorge.* Across the field behind it a wall-stile puts you into the beck's environs. A path runs on the edge of the tree-lined bank, a pleasant amble which, if you miss the turn-off, will lead along to a gate to join the adjacent road. The right of way turn off earlier, where a gate/stile send a track along a fieldside towards the first farm buildings, but joining a back road via a stile just before them. Turn left along this and, keeping left at a junction follow it to its demise at the handful of buildings at what was Leck Mill.

Forking into driveways take the left one, past the house and along to a gate/stile into a field. A cart track heads away through this and a longer field, running along to enter a wood alongside Leck Beck. On emerging, the track runs delightfully on through an extremely long pasture, passing a wooden cabin before reaching a gate/stile at the end. Entering Open Access land, a path traces the beck upstream in very colourful and quite wild country. Though the right of way vacates the beck at the first inflowing stream, a thin path remains with the beck to witness its finest moments. After rounding a slabby corner beneath trees you come upon a wonderful gorge containing several modest but charming waterfalls. At the first and best of these (see page 1) the bed becomes impassable, and the path climbs above: here you emerge onto a slender grassy tongue above an acute angle of the bend. Again high above the beck, a path runs on the bank above before angling back to the once again accessible beck.

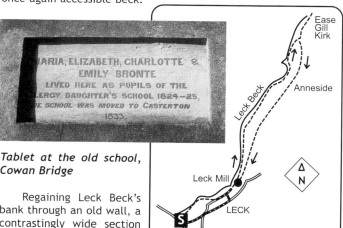

Maria, Elizabeth, Charlotte & Emily Brontë lived here as pupils of the Clergy Daughter's School 1824–25. The school was moved to Casterton 1833.

Tablet at the old school, Cowan Bridge

Regaining Leck Beck's bank through an old wall, a contrastingly wide section is followed below a large curving hollow, until arrival at a sturdy wall. Turn up with it to a ladder-stile on the brow. The route returns to this point after a visit to Ease Gill, now only minutes away. Cross the stile and follow the 'edge' path away through heather. Passing through an old wall the path runs on through rampant bracken to the rim of the ravine of Ease Gill Kirk. *This is a dramatic gorge with sheer lime-stone walls, in normal times dry.* Follow the edge path climbing right to reach some limestone outcrops and more heather. The path continues round above colourful terrain of outcrops, bracken and gnarled trees, cutting back down to a broad, grassy area at a bend above the ravine. To your right is the upper section, which well merits cautious appraisal. *If followed further, the dry bed leads ultimately to Easegill Caves, where the stream of Ease Gill sinks below ground. Here a lovely waterfall tumbles at Cow Holes. At the foot of the Kirk, meanwhile, the stream returns to daylight in lively fashion as Leck Beck.*

To commence the return leave the upper section by heading 'downstream' on the usually dry, stony bed, and when confronted by the dark walls of the main ravine take a thin path up the slope to the left, beneath one small crag and above another to regain the edge path where you first reached it. Return now through the bracken and heather to the ladder-stile. The continuation path keeps to the rim of the escarpment falling towards the outward leg by the beck. After a long-collapsed wall, take the broader left fork to curve around a long pasture to the ruin of Anneside. The track continues by a fence enclosing new tree plantings, then running a decent course along the flank well above older plantations. Fading amid some moist, reedy moments, keep on to a ladder-stile at the very end, where you leave Open Access land. Your way will now simply shadow the right-hand wall all the way back to Leck Mill.

Through a second ladder-stile you enter fields, and a gentle descent starts. *Big views ahead look to the Bowland moors beyond the Wenning Valley, while some grassy banks and ditches on your left indicate the site of an ancient settlement on Castle Hill.* From a stile in the corner continue down to a gate, and with Leck Mill appearing ahead, down to a stream crossing on the valley floor. Ignore a stile in the wall and go on through another gate, then head away to a stone slab crossing of a dry ditch pointing to a corner stile. Resume to the end of the field where a gate puts you back onto the outward route at Leck Mill. If not retracing steps, the quickest return takes the left fork in the road, rising to a crossroads and then turning right - with Leck church spire just to the left - down to the main road.

WHITTINGTON

START Kirkby Lonsdale   Grid ref. SD 615782

DISTANCE 5$\frac{1}{4}$ miles (8$\frac{1}{2}$km)

ORDNANCE SURVEY MAPS
1:50,000
Landranger 97 - Kendal & Morecambe
1:25,000
Explorer OL2 - Yorkshire Dales South/West

ACCESS Start from Devil's Bridge, on the edge of town by the A65. Parking on the old road (west side only at weekends). Served by bus from Lancaster, Kendal and Settle.

> *Easy rambling to an attractive village,
> and a return that clings tightly to the Lune's bank*

Devil's Bridge is a well-known landmark whose three tall, ribbed arches span a lively reach of the Lune. Dating from the late 15th century, its replacement of 1932 left this graceful edifice free of traffic but awash with visitors. A refreshment van enjoys brisk trade. From the town/WC end of the bridge take a stile downstream into the picnic area. At once bear right across to an iron kissing-gate onto the main road. Cross with care to one opposite and rise up the field to one just above. This sends a snicket between houses onto the B6254. Opposite is the fifth kissing-gate in five minutes, from where make a steep ascent of the field. *Pause to look back over the valley backed by Casterton Fell.* On the brow advance on with a slim wood to your left. *Note its densely lichen-covered boulders,* while views to the right look over the town and church tower up the valley to Casterton Fell and Gragareth.

At the far end the path has been diverted: pass through a kissing-gate and on through a second, then pass the farm at Wood End over the wall to a gate just yards short of the corner. Bear right across a small limestone enclosure to a kissing-gate onto the farm drive at a cottage. Cross straight over, passing the cottage to find a splendid enclosed bridleway dropping gently away. A little stream comes in to instil the odd cautious moment when it opts to share the way after rain: the path however largely evades it and as the stream runs into an old millpond, the path bears right to run to a gate into the environs of Sellet Mill. The three-storey former mill stands to the left.

Your route takes a stile on the right, and heads away along the hedgeside as far as a gate in it just past a modern house. Through it cross the field to a gate opposite. *Over to the left rises mighty Ingleborough.* Cross a tiny stream and bear right, joining the hedge to lead along beneath Sellet Bank with the tower of Sellet Hall appearing ahead. As the hedge swings to the left before reaching trees, take a stile in it and head away with the fence outside the wood to reveal the big house just to your left. At the corner rise left to the

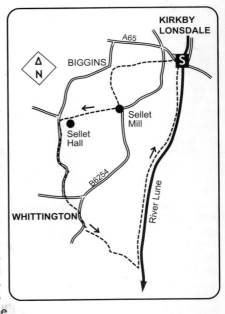

brow and (not quite as per map) drop to a stile in the hedge onto a T-junction. Turn left on the side road for three-quarter mile's traffic-free rambling to Whittington. *Hedgerowed and initially alongside an attractive wood, charmingly named Hosticle Lane gives some open views out to a Bowland skyline.* At the end it drops steeply into the edge of the village.

Go left the few strides to the church, and enter the church-yard by way of an attractive Millennium mosaic. *The parish church of St Michael the Archangel boasts a sturdy 15th century tower. Its distinctive knoll, originally the site of a motte and bailey castle, affords big views over the surrounding countryside. Just off-route along the lane, incidentally, is the lovely Manor House of 1658, with mullioned windows.* Drop down the other side of the knoll to a stile into the lower graveyard, and leave by a gate ahead. The path forks here: keep left with the fence to a kissing-gate, then continue along the fieldside to a squeezer-stile at the far end where a snicket leads out onto Main Street alongside the old school. Turn right to the far end of the village. *En route you pass the Dragons Head pub which incorporates a Post office, and Malt Kiln House of 1687.*

At the far end of the street the road swings right, and a bridle-way turns off left alongside the farm at Low Hall. As Burrow Mill Lane this runs an increasingly pleasant hedgerowed course towards the Lune. *The Bowland moors form the long skyline ahead.* When the lane ultimately turns sharp left over a cattle-grid, bear off right and maintain the same line across the field to a gate in the fence ahead. This suddenly deposits you onto the bank of the River Lune at a long-abandoned ford, with two bungalows at Burrow Mill on the opposite bank. *Immediately upstream is the inflowing Leck Beck.*

Your route is to the left, upstream, quickly passing a wooden anglers' cabin and enjoying a narrow section of path before a stile into a field. *Big views ahead look to Ingleborough, Casterton Fell and Middleton Fell.* Your journey now remains firmly by the Lune all the way back to Devil's Bridge, calling for little further route description. By far the finest section comes when a stile puts you onto a delightful grassy bank at a big pebbly bar. Long strides are enjoyed with a graceful-looking bridge ahead. At the end two neighbouring stiles lead to a gate/stile by the bridge, which on arrival proves to be nothing more exotic than a concrete aqueduct. Slant down past it back to the riverbank and the final section leads ultimately to an iron kissing-gate at the far end of Devil's Bridge's modern replacement on the main road. Re-cross with care to an identical situation opposite, back into the amenity field where you began.

8

WENNING & GRETA

START Melling   Grid ref. SD 598711

DISTANCE 6$\frac{1}{2}$ miles (10$\frac{1}{2}$km)

ORDNANCE SURVEY MAPS
1:50,000
Landranger 97 - Kendal & Morecambe
1:25,000
Explorer OL2 - Yorkshire Dales South/West

ACCESS Start from the village centre. Roadside parking on the Wennington road. Served by Lancaster-Kirkby Lonsdale bus.

> *A richly varied walk encoutering much of interest in between the lower reaches of two parallel rivers*

Melling is a historic Lunesdale village based around the church of St Wilfrid with its solid 15th century tower. Two old milestones are neighbours on the main street, lined by various old houses including a three-storey one of 1774 opposite the church. The large Melling Hall stands at the junction. Head south past the church (using it's yard to avoid the road) and just after the Institute, bear left up an access road. This runs to an open green: don't advance to the house at the end, but bear left up a grass track to the top corner. Don't follow it over the sidestream but take a gate above. *Hutton Roof Crags are seen back over the valley.*

Ascend the fieldside to the next corner gate, which defends a swamp. Escape this and slant slightly right up the big field, a scant line of old trees leading to a gate at the top. *The Dales panorama includes the Howgill Fells, Middleton Fell, Casterton Fell, Crag Hill, Great Coum and Gragareth, joined by Ingleborough: ahead is Bowland.* Now bear right, using stiles to cross several fields to a gate in the hedge on the brow, revealing Lodge Farm just ahead.

34

Pass through the gate (not as per map), down the hedgeside and up to the farm. Pass right of all the buildings, on past the house and down the fieldside. From a stile at the bottom advance over a gentle brow. *This gives fine views ahead into the Wenning Valley, while Ingleborough magnificently dominates its colleagues, including Whernside.* Drop to a gate/stile below, then on again to slant right down to a stile in an outer fence corner before Rectory Wood at the bottom. Follow the fence on your right down towards Tatham church. Bear right in the bottom corner to a small gate onto a driveway. *Note the carved post alongside.* Bear left to the church. *The isolated church of St James the Less dates largely from the 15th century and has a fine old tower.*

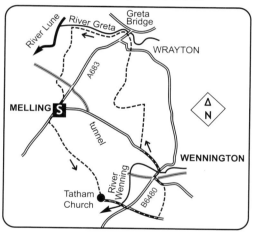

Resume on the hedgerowed road of Monks Gate which runs out to cross Tatham Bridge on the wide River Wenning to join the B6480. *Also bridged is the former Wennington to Lancaster railway, while there is an old weir downstream.* Go left for a few strides, with the Bridge Inn visible just along the road. Your route however turns right down narrow Park Lane, and after a dip begins a stiff ascent. *Back down the valley you can see the prominent Hornby Castle.* This minor lane levels out to pass through a gate into park-like pasture. *To the right is a former schoolhouse of 1875.*

A little further take a stile on the left and cross the field to the skyline trees ahead. A gate sends a path through the short-lived centre to emerge via a stile alongside an old barn: your objective of Overends is just ahead. *Yet another great view has Wennington Hall visible, with Ingleborough dominant as ever.* Drop down the field to a gate/stile and then cross to the farm. Bear right of the main buildings, then left at the end to pass the house and follow the drive away. When it swings sharp right take a gate in front and slant right down the field to a gate/stile in the hedge. Joining Old Moor Lane follow this downhill into Wennington. Bridging the railway to a junction turn right past the station, over the Wenning and into the centre. *Wennington is a peaceful little village based around a central green, alongside which flows the Wenning.*

Turn left on the Melling road, on a footway past further greens and out to Wennington Hall. *Though largely rebuilt in 1856 the building has a long history: it incorporates an impressive square tower, and now serves as a boys' school.* Immediately after, take a small gate on the right and pass through a few trees to a stile. A stiff pull takes you straight up the field centre to the very top. *From this splendid domed viewpoint look over the hall to Bowland, and across to the Dales fells.* From an old stone stile just ahead, head down the field centre to a stile between gates at the bottom. Continue away along a fenceside to a stile onto a hedgerowed track. Turn left on this splendid green lane. *If followed throughout, it leads unfailingly back to Melling for a much shorter conclusion.*

Immediately before opening out at a corner of Melling Moor, leave by a stile on the right, and rise up the fieldside. *This modest brow gives views to the Howgill Fells, Middleton Fell, Casterton Fell, Crag Hill, Great Coum, Gragareth, and awesomely elegant Ingleborough: behind you is Bowland.* Bear right down the other side to a tall gate into trees. A grassy path slants right down through them, past a pond and out via another tall gate. Cross to a gate/stile just ahead from where a cart track heads off through mature trees, leaving them to run a pleasant hedgerowed course out onto the minor road through the hamlet of Wrayton. *An imposing three-storey house stands on the left.*

Go left a few strides to a wall-stile opposite, and an enclosed path runs past the garden at Wrayton Old Hall and down to a stile into a field. Continue down the hedgeside to meet the River Greta at the bottom. Go left outside its bank, briefly, and with a house ahead, bear left over the field to a small gate and steps onto the road at Greta Bridge. *The single stone arch bears the inscription 'Greeta Bridge', and offers the final spanning of the river.* Go briefly right, but instead of crossing use a stile to descend a long flight of stone steps and head downstream with the river. Soon opening out, latch onto a grassy fieldside track before rejoining the riverbank on what proves a good little path.

This runs an improving course through the Greta's final half-mile, a flood bank forming to lead almost to its confluence with the wide-flowing Lune, in view just ahead. The bank however swings left just before this hauntingly peaceful location and along to a gate/stile. Across, advance straight on through scattered trees, the embankment re-forming to offer a splendid walk along its straight course. Passing a reedy pool a fence corner is reached, leading along to a gate onto a hedgerowed cart track. Turn right on this (tiresome when churned up by farm vehicles) which runs on to an underpass beneath the Leeds-Morecambe railway. Beneath, turn left and follow the track out, absorbing a drive and leading out to the main road on the edge of the village. Turn right to finish, with a footway forming.

St James the Less, Tatham

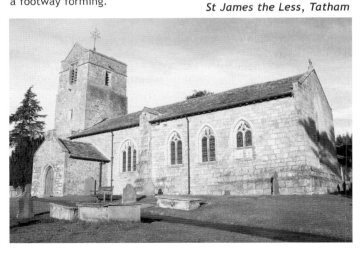

THREE RIVERS

START *Hornby   Grid ref. SD 585683*

DISTANCE *5¹2 miles (9km)*

ORDNANCE SURVEY MAPS
1:50,000
Landranger 97 - Kendal & Morecambe
1:25,000
Explorer OL41 - Forest of Bowland & Ribblesdale

ACCESS *Start from the village centre, car park on the south side of the bridge. Served by Lancaster-Kirkby Lonsdale bus.*

> *Two absorbing, very contrasting villages link the genteel Lune Valley with the wilder, wooded edge of Bowland*

   Hornby is an elegant village split by the wide Wenning rolling through for its final mile before it enters the Lune. St Margaret's church has an intriguing octagonal tower of 1514 courtesy of Edward Stanley, Lord Monteagle of Hornby Castle. Opposite is St Mary's Roman Catholic church. Aside from the Royal Oak pub is a Post office, shop and butchers. Hornby also has a high school and fire station, while an old milestone stands opposite the derelict Castle Hotel. Best-known feature is the Lune Valley landmark of Hornby Castle, which has a long and colourful history. Originally a Norman structure, Cromwell rendered it unfortified after the Civil War. Rebuilt in the mid-19th century, an early 16th century tower survives. In residential use, it is best seen from the bridge.
   From the big, wide bridge head a few yards south and take a short lane on the left, on the near side of the Institute. Pass through a gate into a farmyard and follow the concrete road to the bank of the Wenning. *There is a first sighting of Ingleborough*

straight ahead. This runs upstream, and as the river bends off, the track runs on through the field. *There is a good view back to the castle rising above the wooded bank*. At the end pass through a gate and take one on the right to a muddy bridge on a stream. Cross straight over the field to a stile, then bear left to the next and maintain this distinct course with stiles linking several fields to meet a wall. *Over it is the former railway opened in 1850 to link the West Riding towns with Morecambe, but this section between Wennington and Lancaster closed to passenger traffic in 1966.*

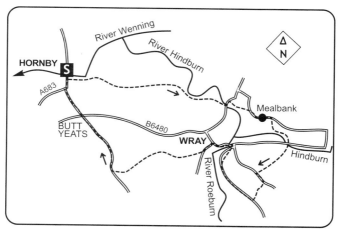

Go left on a grassy wallside track to a track crossroads at the end. Cross the old line on your right by kissing-gates, and head off on a hedgerowed green way. At its end take a kissing-gate, with the River Hindburn just ahead. Go along the field edge to pick up a grass track at a gate, and on again, briefly, until a stile in the hedge on the left keeps you by the river. From the next stile however cross to the sewage works, where a short enclosed path outside its perimeter puts you onto its access track. Go left on this past the entrance and keep on, a broad hedgerowed way running along to the modern bridge at Meal Bank on the B6480 on the edge of Wray.

Cross the bridge and just along the verge take a stile on the right. Briefly following a green way left, quickly turn uphill for a short pull to a stile at the top. Head away with a line of trees pointing to a prominent stile in a hedge ahead. From it bear left up to Meal Bank Farm, taking a stile to the left to run out onto a back road at the farm entrance. Turn right for a couple of minutes to the next farm, Far Mealbank, and after the house pass through the yard to a gate at the back into a field. *In front is the richly wooded Hindburn Valley, with Bowland beyond.* Head away, dropping to a small gate onto a steep little bank. Descend to a gateway, taking a gate on the left to follow a track around the rear of the house at Gamblesholme and out between barns to the front. Head away on its access track high above the Hindburn to meet a road at Hindburn Bridge. *Fine river scenery features low cliffs upstream.*

Across the bridge take a small gate in front and ascend to a stile into Powley Wood. Noting a grand little waterfall, a thin path bears right, slanting up above the field and then rising away through the trees leading out to rise gently to a kissing-gate at the top. Emerging into a field head directly away with the hedge, over a gentle brow. *Ahead is the Bowland skyline, while gentle views look across the Lune Valley to find the Coniston Fells looking quite distinctive.* From a gate at the end you emerge onto another back road in front of an old barn. *The Dales skyline leads from the Howgill Fells around to Whernside.*

An old cottage doorway at Wray

Go briefly left then bear right down a hedgerowed green way, dropping grandly into the trees of Pike Gill Wood and along by Hunt's Gill Beck to an old ford and a footbridge. *This is a grand spot as the beck tumbles over rocky slabs.* A steep, hollowed way climbs the other side, doubling back right up the bank to a gate in front of Alcocks Farm onto another back road. *On a clear day keen eyes will locate the Lakeland giants of Crinkle Crags and Bowfell to the right of the Coniston Fells.* Turn right on this to descend through trees to re-cross Hunt's Gill Beck and find the River Roeburn for company on your left. Just beyond is a renovated former bobbin mill and a row of millworkers' cottages. Remain on the road by the river to a junction at Wray Bridge, though at the end of the wood on your right note a stile sending a short-cut fieldpath to stone steps at the end of a short terrace.

Built about 1780, Wray Bridge withstood the floods that wreaked havoc after a freak cloudburst on the moors in August 1967, causing the river to rise 20 feet in 20 minutes. Its sturdiness only increased damage as water banked up, and the little green caught the full fury of the devastation. A garden by surviving Bridge End is on the site of five houses that fell victim out of a row of six. To the right is Bridge House Farm, with visitor centre, café and gifts. Wray and the Roeburn are indelibly linked, the river having supplied water power for an industrious past: like the adjacent Hindburn, it is named from the deer that roamed the Forest of Bowland. Attractive cottages line the streets, including many old yeoman houses: one inscribed 'RP 1656' refers to Richard Pooley who founded the school. Holy Trinity church dates from 1840, with the Church House of 1694 alongside: nearby is an ornate street lamp commemorating Queen Victoria's Golden Jubilee in 1887. There is a Post office/shop and a Friends' Meeting House of 1704. Central pub is the George & Dragon, with a second, the Inn at Wray, on the main road. A popular local event is the Maytime scarecrow festival.

Go left over the bridge and along the street to a junction just before the church. Turn left here up School Lane, climbing steeply past the school to a bend. *Look back over the village roofs to the Wenning Valley backed by the fells of Three Peaks Country.* Take a gate on the right and head across the field, rising above the wall to a stile at the end. Continue on, passing above attractive Neddy

WALK 9 • THREE RIVERS

Park Wood. At the end go to a stile above the corner, and away along a fenceside rising to a brow. *Looking back, the Dales peak of Penyghent presents a shapely profile along with Ingleborough.* From a myriad gate arrangement at the end, keep straight on with a fence now on your right. Follow this all the way to the end where a stile puts you onto a minor road, Moor Lane.

Turn right on this, over a slight brow. *Hornby Castle is seen ahead in front of Hutton Roof Crags.* The lane drops to a seat alongside an impressive old roadside cross at a farm drive. *Ingleborough rises beyond, and views to the fells remain good for most of this descent.* Resuming, the lane drops all the way down to a crossroads with the B6480 at Butt Yeats. *Note the big stone cross base.* Cross straight over along Station Road and a roadside footway leads along, over the former rail bridge (past the old station site) and back into Hornby. *A fountain of 1858 stands at the junction.*

Hornby Castle from the Wenning

THE BENTHAMS

START *Burton-in-Lonsdale   Grid ref. SD 651721*

DISTANCE *6¼ miles (10km)*

ORDNANCE SURVEY MAPS
1:50,000
Landranger 97 - Kendal & Morecambe
Landranger 98 - Wensleydale & Upper Wharfedale
1:25,000
Explorer OL2 - Yorkshire Dales South/West

ACCESS *Start from the village centre. Roadside parking. Served by Lancaster-Ingleton bus.*

A rolling landscape of hedgerowed fields and villages between Bowland and the Three Peaks: the only walk in North Yorkshire

Burton-in-Lonsdale is an independent village, on the bank of the River Greta rather than in Lonsdale. Rising above the green is the tall-spired church of All Saints, dating from 1870. Immediately to its west are the distinctive mounds of a motte and bailey castle site. As well as the Punch Bowl Inn, Burton has a community-run Post office/shop, a Methodist church of 1871 and numerous old cottages with dated lintels. The village was once known as Black Burton due to the amount of smoke emitted by its vast number of potteries, an industry at its peak in the 1800s.

From the centre descend the Bentham road to cross the three-arched bridge on the Greta. Ascend the road climbing steeply away, and at the top look back to see the village dominated by its church. From a gate/stile on the left head diagonally away to a stile at the top end of a wooded clough, then rise up the field bearing left to a stile. *Ahead is a first sighting of the Bowland moors.*

From this brow on what was once Bentham Moor you have bigger views left to the fells of Three Peaks Country, dominated, as they always will be, by Ingleborough. Bear further left to a corner stile, then on to a ladder-stile framed by stiles a short way either side. Head away with a hedge on your right masking a large greenhouse complex. From a stile at the end an enclosed path encounters a brief swampy moment to reach a stile onto a road.

Cross straight over and away up a hedgerowed cart track. *At a mere 400ft/122m high its brow is the summit of the walk, and reveals much more of Bowland ahead.* Dropping down to a gate/stile into a field bear left, over a slight brow. *Ingleborough looks typically awesome to the left.* Head on through an intervening gate/stile, and on above a hedge corner on the left to slant down into a trough. At the

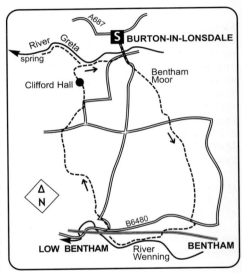

end is a stile from where the ways fork. Ignore the slab bridge to your left and advance along the fieldside, still in a pleasant trough. At the end another slab bridge takes you over the tiny stream, then climb steeply left to a gate/stile. Advance on with the hedge on your left, with Haybers barn up to your right. Keep on with the hedge, swinging right to drop to a corner stile. Dropping to a dip, ignore a wall-stile and ascend to another stile. Remain with the hedge along to a stile and steps down onto the road at the western edge of High Bentham. Go briefly left on the footway to a bend in front of the Horse & Farrier pub.

The centre of Bentham (properly High Bentham) is just along the road. This bustling old market town is hub of the Wenning Valley and marks the northern limit of Bowland. Its true colours are shown by being part of Yorkshire, and its surroundings offer tantalizing panoramas of the mountains of Three Peaks Country. This western outpost of England's premier county is situated just a dozen miles from Morecambe Bay. Shops and pubs abound, and livestock and street markets survive.

Immediately before the pub double back right along Duke Street, passing an intriguing mullioned windowed house. Quickly entering an open area take the rough road right, past the rear of a short terrace. When it swings left past them take a stile in front, and head away with a wall. From a stile/steps at the end continue along the field top, with a large caravan park down by the river. When the hedge turns off advance to a kissing-gate sending an enclosed path running parallel with the Leeds-Morecambe railway line of 1850. At the end cross the line to another kissing-gate onto a broad path immediately overlooking the River Wenning. Turn briefly right, then take a kissing-gate to commence a popular riverside walk. This runs a splendid course downstream, an early S-bend being especially nice where it spills over low ledges. Further downstream the path is deflected away from the river on an enclosed course past a fishery to meet the railway again. Pass under the arch and along to the main road through Low Bentham.

Though subservient to its near neighbour, Low Bentham is a colourful little village with much of interest. A little out of the centre an area by the river comprises church, pub and school: the architecturally intriguing church of St John the Baptist occupies a historic site but apart from the centuries-old tower was largely rebuilt in the 1870s, while alongside are the Punch Bowl Inn and the old grammar school, now part of Sedbergh School. Turn briefly right towards the Victoria Institute and Public Hall of 1804, but fork left past the Sun Dial Inn, complete with said timepiece (see page 3). Advance along the street past the Post office/shop and Wesleyan Chapel of 1886. When the road swings sharp right go straight ahead on Greenfoot Lane to a small green. *On it stands a monument to the coronation of Edward VII in 1902.* Follow the road climbing to a bend, and ignoring the rough road heading left, go just a few yards right on Cross Lane then turn up a drive to the house at Green Head Farm. Just past it is a gate from where a hedgerowed green way heads off, with big views of Ingleborough.

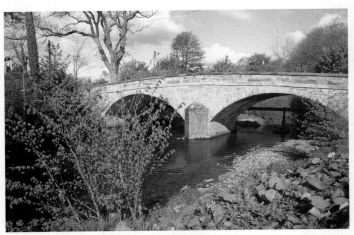

Punch Bowl Bridge on the Wenning, Low Bentham

Remain on this track to its demise, soon absorbing but then losing a rougher farm track. It swings left amid plentiful hollies and along to emerge into a field. Cross to a stile in the moist corner just ahead to enter a large, rolling pasture. Bear right to a stile midway along the fence, then head directly away. Passing left of a solitary oak, then a wooded hollow, advance to a gate in the hedge ahead onto a road. Go a few yards right to a stile in the hedge opposite, and slant right up the field to reach an outer hedge corner on the brow. *This is the walk's finest viewpoint as the foreground, which includes Burton church, falls away to present a superb panorama from Casterton Fell to Ingleborough by way of Middleton Fell, Crag Hill, Gragareth and Whernside. Far to the left, a long Lakeland skyline culminates in the distinctive outline of the Langdale Pikes.*

Maintain the slant down to a corner stile in the hedge below. This puts you back on a road: go briefly left to a bend then keep left on Clifford Hall Farm drive. Approaching a modern residential hamlet, drop down to a pond in front and along their drive between the houses: when it swings left behind the first ones, take a path straight ahead between gardens, rising back onto the farm drive. This runs to the farm just ahead, but you bear right on a cart track into the top of a wood. It runs on to quickly expire towards the edge, but a good path doubles back right down into the heart of the wood. Levelling out, with the river just below, a thinner but clear path turns off left. This offers a splendid walk to visit the chalybeate spring marked on the map: you will return to this point.

The thinner path contours downstream to quickly reach a stile out of the trees, and an intermittent path continues above the bank. *This is a truly super walk through delightful surroundings: from this colourful pasture you look over gorgeous river scenery of rocky slabs and walls to a richly wooded bank.* 150 yards beyond a miry pool is a stile into more woodland. Strictly the right of way ends here, but just 100 yards further the continuing anglers' path runs past the chalybeate spring. *Emerging from beneath a rocky wall just to the left, the waters show themselves immediately under the boardwalk path, their rich iron colour unmistakable.* Return to the main path and resume above the bank upstream, soon passing into the Woodland Trust's Greta Wood. A little further the path leaves the river to run between gardens to join a drive, leading out onto a back road. This runs with the scenic river back to the bridge just ahead. Re-cross and re-ascend into the village.

Motte and Bailey, Burton-in-Londale

LOWER LUNESDALE

START *Caton*   *Grid ref. SD 521648*

DISTANCE *7^{1}2 miles (12km)*

ORDNANCE SURVEY MAPS
1:50,000
Landranger 97 - Kendal & Morecambe
1:25,000
Explorer OL41 - Forest of Bowland & Ribblesdale

ACCESS Start from Crook o'Lune car park on the north side of Caton Lune Bridge. Crook o'Lune is not actually named on the map, though its location is obvious on the edge of Caton. Caton is served by bus from Lancaster, Kirkby Lonsdale and Ingleton.

A lengthy stroll on the banks of the wide-flowing Lune, and a return through open fields on the colourful flanks high above

The Crook o'Lune is a place of popular resort, the crook itself being a very distinctive sharp bend in the River Lune. A stone-arched bridge crosses one section, while a pair of rail viaducts straddles both. The road bridge, Caton Lune Bridge was rebuilt in 1880, having earlier been a toll bridge known as Penny Bridge: to add further confusion it is also known as Crook o'Lune Bridge. The railway line opened in 1850 to connect the West Riding towns with Morecambe, but this section between Wennington and Lancaster closed to passenger traffic in 1966. A scenic length was purchased by an enterprising local authority, and today the section from Lancaster as far as Caton is a much-used bridleway.

From the car park descend steps to the old railway line. Don't cross the viaduct but take a path on the left down to the riverbank. From a gate a path heads upstream on the open grassy bank. *From these very pleasant open surrounds numerous landmarks come into view: Caton Moor windfarm is the unnatural addition to Ward's Stone and Clougha, further right, while mighty Ingleborough makes a more enduring landmark straight ahead.* After a couple of long pastures a stile puts you into woodland, and a good path runs along the base to re-emerge into open pasture. A gentle river bend is cut by remaining near the wooded bank to reach a footbridge on a sidestream. The river is rejoined to reach the Waterworks Bridge. *This massive aqueduct was built by Manchester Corporation Water Works to carry Lakeland water from Thirlmere to the thirsty city. It carries a concession path, should you desire a speedy return down the opposite bank.*

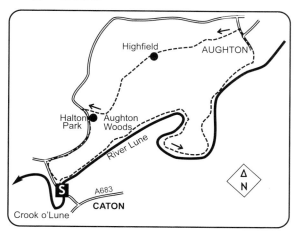

Just beyond it a stile and footbridge put you into Aughton Woods. *This is a reserve of the Lancashire, Manchester & North Merseyside Wildlife Trust, and sports a delightful bluebell display in spring.* A good path runs through, rising a little from the bank before leaving via a step-stile at the end. Here you become aware of the river undertaking a mighty loop, which your route will trace. *Though people regularly take a short-cut by remaining outside the wooded bank to pick up the returning river a little ahead, there is no official right of way. The riverbank hereabouts is a haven for birdlife, notably waders.*

On the riverbank, meanwhile, the way swings right to cross a stile into a ploughed field, to angle back to a scrubby riverbank fence. *You're now heading down-valley, but walking upstream!* Crossing a footbridge on a sidestream just ahead, path and fence soon close in on the river. Surroundings improve still further after swinging back left through a gate/stile into open pasture. Trace the bank until deflected from it on approaching sturdy Over Lune Barn. Passing this isolated building the way follows the crest of an embankment, through a gate some way from the river, swinging right as the embankment fades to cross to rejoin the Lune. *Ahead, a fine skyline of Dales heights features Crag Hill, Great Coum, Gragareth, Whernside and Ingleborough: Hornby Castle is beneath.*

Resume a grand stride upstream, over an intervening stile and noting a track forming to the left. Reaching sheep pens it is time to leave the river: ignore a stile in front in favour of a gate/stile just to the left by the pens, as the track passes through and leads to the cottages at Aughton Barns. Here an access road forms to give a punishing ascent through the woodland of Aughton Brow before running into the tranquil hamlet of Aughton. *Pronounced 'Afton', a tiny sloping green sports a seat on which to recover. The Old Hall stands behind, while spring flowers decorate the scene.*

Continue uphill for a couple of minutes to an iron ladder-stile on the left: from it bear right to a gate/stile. *Big sweeping views look over the valley to Bowland's moors.* Maintain the slant up a large field to another old stile in the very top corner, as Far Highfield farm appears ahead. *Pause here to look back to the peaks of the Dales, now joined by their westernmost member, Middleton Fell.* Beyond a footbridge cross to a stile just left of the buildings, a potentially messy corner. Head away from the farm, merging with a fence on the right to an outer corner. In much improved terrain head away with the fence on your right, encountering a stile with a benchmarked gatepost and a redundant ladder-stile, and tracing an old hedge to approach Middle Highfield. From a stile at the end, cross a smaller enclosure to pass through the yard, then through a gap in front of the farmhouse to a narrow little way onto an access track. Cross straight over to a wall-stile and along a tiny cobbled snicket to emerge onto an access road amid a modern residential development. *On the left is a former chapel at Highfield House.* Go briefly left to the road end and take a gate/stile on your right.

Bear right down the open field to merge with a wall, and beyond a gate in a dip follow this 7-foot monster away, continuing with a fence to a gate/stile at the far end. Cross to a hedge-gap in front, then slant right down to a hedgerow dropping gently all the way to Lower Highfield. Keep on to a gate in the far corner, left of the farm buildings. Drop down through the yard and down to a lower yard, observing the interesting house to your right. At the bottom a gate sends a track down to a stream crossing and gate. Cross the field bottom to an iron kissing-gate into the wood ahead. A path rises along the wood edge, then on through the part-felled centre to a gate out the other side. *This gives super views over the valley, with Caton itself outspread below.*

Cross the big, sloping field to a fence corner and head along the hedgeside, a grand stride soon revealing the mansion of Halton Park below. On starting to drop down, take a pair of stiles on your right to resume, dropping down to a stile immediately after the farm buildings of Hawkshead. Emerging onto the drive, turn right as it winds down through trees onto a through road, Park Lane. Amble pleasantly left, swinging round past Halton Park and its farm, then down through woodland to emerge into a big, sloping pasture. Trace the verge along to a T-junction. Its narrow footway can be eschewed in favour of an all-purpose trail that runs a parallel course along the field-edges, leading quickly back to the car park.

The River Lune at Aughton Woods

51

12

CROOK O'LUNE

START Halton   Grid ref. SD 503645

DISTANCE 6¹2 miles (10¹2km)

ORDNANCE SURVEY MAPS
1:50,000
Landranger 97 - Kendal & Morecambe
1:25,000
Explorer OL41 - Forest of Bowland & Ribblesdale

ACCESS Start from Lune Riverside Walk car park at the old station, on the south side of the river off the A683 at Denny Bank just east of the M6 junction. Served by bus from Lancaster.

> Simple rambling on the Lune's banks and a former railway line

   Halton village is encountered at the end of the walk. Its red-brick former station differs from others on the line as it was rebuilt in 1907 after being set on fire by a passing train. The line itself opened in 1850 to connect the West Riding towns with Morecambe, but this section between Wennington and Lancaster closed to passenger traffic in 1966. A scenic length was purchased by an enterprising local authority, and today the section from Lancaster as far as Caton is a much-used bridleway. From the station you have the immediate option to simply follow the surfaced trackbed: nicer though is an initial riverbank path, running through the trees and passing a wide weir. Very soon however the going toughens, and reaching a stone rail embankment a flight of steps takes you up onto the line. *Attempts to continue are thwarted by desperate manouevres on the riverbank.* Following the trail there is soon chance to tread a soft path on the left. When this briefly fades but soon starts again, this time take another path slanting down, not reaching the river but running a grand, mid-level course. At the end it drops to the very bank by a wide, curving weir, and a stile puts you onto an access track serving the weir. Don't follow it but bear right of the enclosure to regain the riverbank.

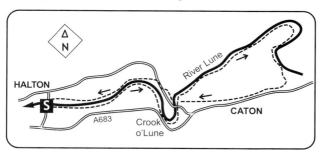

A good path runs on through trees and over some ground-level tanks where you again ignore an access road climbing away. From a stile in front a super section begins, tracing the open, grassy bank around through verdant loveliness with tall wooded banks across the calm water. The river swings right to take the path into trees, with Crook o'Lune western rail viaduct just ahead. Ignoring steps up to join the line, remain true to the riverbank and pass under the arch. A good path resumes through Low Mill Wood, soon ascending to the top. At a path junction keep left, parallel with the main road just above, and soon more steps return you to the foot of the wood at the Crook o'Lune itself. *As you curve round before leaving the wood, the acute angle of the crook reveals both the old viaduct downstream and the road bridge upstream.*

A stile out of the trees sends a path on through an amenity area to a kissing-gate onto the road alongside the bridge. *The Crook o'Lune is a place of popular resort. A stone-arched bridge crosses one section, while a pair of rail viaducts straddles both. The road bridge, Caton Lune Bridge was rebuilt in 1880, having earlier been a toll bridge known as Penny Bridge: to add further confusion it is also known by many as Crook o'Lune Bridge.* Cross to a bridle-gate opposite, and instead of following the hard path to the old railway line, drop left to the riverbank to find a path squeezing beneath the eastern viaduct.

Immediately through, a delectable riverbank path heads upstream, enjoying wide open spaces. *Look over the wide-flowing river to lovely wooded banks, and upstream to Ingleborough and across right to Low Mill, Caton Moor windfarm, Ward's Stone and Clougha Pike.* Passing a weir before crossing a substantial curved footbridge on Artle Beck, the bank leads to the Waterworks Bridge. *This massive aqueduct was built by Manchester Corporation Water Works to carry Lakeland water from Thirlmere to the thirsty city.* Beyond it is a seat with lovely views across the Lune to Aughton Woods. Through a kissing-gate just beyond comes the finest section, a delectable greensward that leads you to a great loop of the river. Not that obvious until you reach it, it becomes very obvious that there's little option but to double back right to head down-valley, yet still upstream! Through a kissing-gate level with the previous one, the way curves delightfully round to the loop, and on to reach a cattle feeding station. A track forms and leads past animal pens and a little further before leaving the river. Becoming enclosed by hedgerows it runs pleasantly along to a lone house, just past which it meets the old railway just yards short of the A683.

Turn right on the track, running parallel with the main road around the back of the village. After bridging Artle Beck again it reaches a kink at Caton's old Station House and a Roman Catholic church. *A half-minute detour left on Station Road puts you in the village centre. Caton is a busy little village with two pubs, the Ship Inn and the Station, and a Post office/shop. The parish church of St Paul stands in neighbouring Brookhouse, as that was then the real Caton!*

Station House, Caton

The trail runs on to return to the first half of its double crossing of the Lune. *Easiest option is to remain on it all the way back to the start.* After crossing, turn right up steps into Crook o'Lune car park, with WC. At the right edge of the car park by picnic tables, a firm track heads off through a gate, curving around (with big views over the river) to a path junction alongside a road. Cross to the footway and go a few yards right, where an iron kissing-gate sends a path slanting down a wooded bank to rejoin the river.

On through the trees it emerges via a small footbridge into the scrubby banks of a colourful no-man's-land. At a fork remain on the lower path to re-enter woodland at the end. Overlooking the wide, curving weir again, the path forks. Drop left down wooden steps to the weir-edge, and resume downstream on the bank. A rough road leads past old quarries to the unkempt environs of largely derelict Halton Mills. Keep on, merging into Mill Lane which leads out past new housing. Look out for a path appearing on the adjacent grass, overlooking the Lune and the first weir. The path leaves the river to rejoin Mill Lane, which just ahead joins Station Road in Halton.

Halton is a mixture of old village with interesting buildings around the church, and modern commuter additions elsewhere. It has a pub, the Greyhound. St Wilfrid's church has a 16th century tower and two-storey porch. Turn left to cross the narrow iron and concrete Halton Bridge to finish. *Erected in 1911, it was recycled from an 1864 rail bridge in Lancaster. Visible downstream is the M6.*

The River Lune at Crook o'Lune

INDEX *(walk number refers)*

WALK LOG

WALK	DATE	NOTES
1		
2		
3		
4		
5		
6		
7		
8		
9		
10		
11		
12		